CAPE POETRY PAPERBACKS

Wish You Were Here

Adrian Henri

10.iv.92.

by the same author

TONIGHT AT NOON
CITY
THE MERSEY SOUND
(with Roger McGough and Brian Patten)
I WANT
(with Nell Dunn)
AUTOBIOGRAPHY
ENVIRONMENTS AND HAPPENINGS
THE BEST OF HENRI
CITY HEDGES
FROM THE LOVELESS MOTEL
PENNY ARCADE

Wish You Were Here

ADRIAN HENRI

JONATHAN CAPE
LONDON

First published 1990
Reprinted 1990
© Adrian Henri 1990
Jonathan Cape Ltd, 20 Vauxhall Bridge Road,
London SW1V 2SA

A CIP catalogue record for this book is available
from the British Library

ISBN 0 224 02778 6

A number of these poems began life, usually in slightly different form, as commissions, including 'For Joyce Henri, New Year 1988' for Freeway Films' New Year 1988 programme for Channel Four TV, 'City Nocturne' for The City of London Festival and 'Morning, Liverpool 8' for BBC TV's 'Venice of the North'. The 40 lines of 'The Birthday Party' were commissioned by Annie Russell for Willy Russell's fortieth birthday, and 'Shadowland' uses themes from Adrian Henri's narrative poems for 'Fears and Miseries of the Third Term' devised by Kate Rowland for Liverpool Playhouse. Some of the poems have appeared in *Ambit* magazine. 'Holiday Snaps' was published by 'Windows' as a Merseyside Poetry Minibook in 1985.

The four lines in the dedication for 'The Long and Wider Road' on page 13 are from *The Road is Wider than Long* by Roland Penrose, published by London Gallery Editions in 1939 and reissued by the Arts Council of Great Britain in 1980.

Typeset by Hope Services (Abingdon) Ltd.
Printed and bound in Great Britain by
Mackays of Chatham, PLC, Chatham, Kent

For Joyce Henri
née Wilson
1935–1987

Contents

For Joyce Henri, New Year 1988

In 1987
Willy was 40, Roger was 50, I was 55 and you
were 52. We drank fizzy wine at your bedside
knowing you wouldn't see 53.
In 1987
sailors died
killed by missiles fired by people not their enemies
sold them by their fellow-countrymen;
blood mocked the colour of poppies
once more in the November mist,
and I
made my usual Autumn note in my notebook
about willowherb.
In 1987
I saw
our remembered tree-filled square
in Preston. The school I worked in
now a wine-bar. A shopping-arcade
across the backstreets where we kissed.
I saw
walnuts fall from a walnut-tree
silently through the memory;
stocks and shares fall
like horse-chestnuts:
no laughing children
rushed to pick them from the floor
of the Stock Exchange. Only pigeons, they said,
could leave a deposit on a Porsche.
On July afternoons
we watched Australian soaps, quiz-programmes,
you propped up in your nightdress.
I brought you old-fashioned sweets,
Treacle Toffees, Jap Desserts, Pontefract Cakes.
In 1987
people took a ferry
across the darkest river
or an escalator

to the underworld
and didn't return.
The clatter of a Kalashnikov
tore through the postcard of an English village.
In Beirut
dying was Business As Usual.
She wore winceyette pyjamas like a child,
laughed with me in Liverpool, Edinburgh, Strasbourg,
Paris, and cried for you in London, though
she didn't know you. Strands of dark hair
in every kiss. Late leaves
in the Cathedral square.

And you died
not in bleak midwinter
but a rainy August.
The sun shone on Smithdown Cemetery
when we buried you. Sue and I
worried about who would want what,
the scrap-screen, the books, the rocking-chair.
In 1987
a small boy cried at my side
when twin brothers died
in the theatre. In the real world outside
I didn't cry for you.

Will it be too late
in 1988?

Tea with the Poet

We are going to tea with a poet.
Confidences poured out –
'One lump or two? Milk?'
– and passed round the table.
Hot toasted paragraphs
dripping with melted adjectives,
sentences with the crusts neatly cut off,
a tempting selection of metaphors –
'Must watch the figure'
– laid out on a plate for us to choose from.

It is teatime with the poet.
'A second cup? Certainly.
Pass the haiku. A villanelle?
Go on, spoil yourself.
Sure you haven't got room for a sonnet?
Oh, very well.'

Time to go.
He brushes up a few commas from the tablecloth
and, with a polite semi-colon;
shows us to the door.

Garden, Giverny

Delphiniums, sweet williams,
purple gladioli,
against yellow asters, marigolds,
the whirl of sunflowers;
glimpsed pink walls against emerald shutters.

A bamboo-grove
lurks in the shadows by the lily-pond,
patient as a tiger.
Lovers kiss on a Japanese bridge
watched by the bearded phantom
from behind the willows,
sad as a blind girl in a summer garden.

Harbour, Cullercoats

Desire comes
regular as the flash of the lighthouse,
the sound of a foghorn,
the rhythm of sea against seawall.
Your image
persistent as the battered coaster through the mist,
the grey silhouette of the priory,
a red warning-light
against the grey sea.
The stealth of salt
slow corruption beneath the gaudy colours
its faint trace on my lips
the remembered taste of you.

Liverpool Poems

1

White
under the orange lights
a rabbit
lopes along Hope St.
at 3 a.m.

2

a Hardman St. wino
demands money from a man
getting out of a van
marked WAR ON WANT.

3

'If I cannot do great things
I will do small things in a great way'
the kitten on the poster says
above her neat grey head
as she signs the death-certificate.

4

a plump young pigeon
dying in Rodney St.
whistles as ineffectually
as the tramp with the penny whistle on the corner.

5

in St. Luke's gardens a drunk rises from a urine-splashed
    bench
lurches across the neat grass with total concentration
to pick an orange geranium.

6

the last throes of summer
reflected blinding from the river
at the foot of the hill
the first hint of October
stirs poems along the cobbled street.

Morning, Belfast

for the girls of St. Louisa's, Belfast

Brown-uniformed
blue-ribboned
Children of Mary
Siobhan and Maureen,
Mary and Siobhan
your faces should adorn
the gable-ends of walls
ten feet high along the Falls.

City Nocturne

The day
hurries past St. Vedast's
through to St. Andrew Undershaft.
A skein of light threads its way
along Threadneedle Street,
then past the feet of Rowland Hill;
still air where starlings call
from Ludgate to Guildhall.
From Leadenhall to Spitalfields
the City yields up the day.
St. Mary-le-Bow, St. Mary Somerset,
St. Mary Woolnoth, all go into the dark.
In square and park the shadows
wait. The monument, the spires
touched with tongues of fire.
The night
levels its eyes like a gunman
aims fires:
another city bites the dusk.

Hotel

Amid tropical decor
they laugh in evening dress
and speak of markets, of orders lost
and gained. I sit
in my fluorescent scarf and socks
as fans revolve overhead
and try to graph the ebb and flow
of your feelings, anticipate
the profit and loss of our loving.

Alice/Early Autumn

Sunshine
overtaken by the shingle-sound
of first leaves along Hope Street
the tinkle of a Coke-can
a black plastic bag
slinks along the gutter.

In London,
uniformed toddlers play ring o' roses
in leafstrewn squares
a pale brown cat
among cat-coloured leaves
on the lawn.

Your smile
across the water of the ornamental pond
like a mayfly in October.

Alice in Winter

It is New Year's Day, and the Year of the Rabbit.
We wake to the distant sound of firecrackers,
the beat of drums and cymbals.
Down the hill the Dragon capers, leaps,
flutters gilded eyelids, eats
the lettuce-leaves, the bright red messages
dangled from windows by laughing children.
I burrow into you in the darkness,
close brown warren of the bedclothes.

Later we follow his footsteps,
torn lettuce-leaves, red messages
trodden underfoot.
Spent firecrackers thick as beech-mast
on the wet pavement.

The Long and Wider Road
Elegiac fragments for Roland Penrose

'If you are lying your finger will be trapped
If you tell the truth it will lead you
out to the other side
                    to an island'
                    — Roland Penrose 'The Road is Wider than Long'

I

Autumn destroys:
a shadow
pushes itself across the garden
the mingled smell of chestnuts and excrement
cars trapped in tunnels
patient as rats on a dissecting-table
glimpsed dimples
in the midst of traffic-jams
the road
longer than wide
hurtling landscape into white landscape.

2

A pipe without a name
that proclaims
THIS IS NOT MYSELF
shelf of forgotten expectations
discovered cupboard
of discarded dreams.

3

Miserable miracle
that sits just out of sight,
crawls in spidertrails
against the light,
lurks
at the edge of comprehension.

4

Erotic phantom just down the street
shrouded in bright blue honeysuckle
veil briefly lifted,
tantalized by the lamplight;
DESIRE written in the stars
reflected sudden in her eyes.

5

THIS IS NOT A POEM
screams the poem
soundlessly.

Honeysuckle

For fourteen years he loved her from
four doors away. After seven years
she planted honeysuckle at her door.
Often, returning drunk, its smell
would turn the night to poetry. Her image
at the back of his mind, persistent
as a rhymescheme. One year
she gave him honeysuckle soap
for Christmas. Her husband asked him round
for drinks. After the honeysuckle,
two children, who grew as quickly.
Soon her family will move away,
scented vines abandoned. Tonight,
she lies in his arms, palpable as syllables,
soft as nightsmelling flowers, promises herself
within four years. Outside her bright blue door
unattended tendrils wither in the first frost.

Friday Morning, Early October

'One thing might lead
to another'
you say. 'Better not meet
another day.' On the morning
telephone. Alone,
and wondering,
what thing led us
to one another. What thing
will lead you to another.

Letter

a letter from you
on the morning doormat
unexpected
as a rainbow over Runcorn.

Remembrance Sunday, Cheltenham

Crimson and yellow chrysanthemums
stand to attention
orange leaves swirled by the sound of brass
on the eleven o'clock wind.

Sunday Morning

After Beethoven we lie, exhausted,
my head against your thigh. The audience
cheers. Storms of applause. My
mouth against yours. Now
Part Two begins. Brahms. I lie
in your arms.

sunset
Heights

HOLIDAY SNAPS

for Lis

'black marigolds
in the desert of a long-lost summer'

In the empty streets of this city
it is 9.35 and the images are dying
beneath broken barriers at football-stadiums
inside television sets everywhere

Lost in the dark Mogodon forests
of morning. The whirring of a milk float
an electric mole humming to itself
in the darkness. The little pig you made me
three Christmases ago still stands
on the bedside table. The cassette-alarm
that alarmed us to Pastoral mornings,
dawn Rhine journeys, stolen.
Only the travelling alarm-clock
that follows me everywhere remains,
faithful as Greyfriars Bobby.

I

Sunset Heights:
heaped-up
cactus, ground-ivy,
white walls, hibiscus
and cypresses
piled stark up
against implacable blue.

2

At Universal Studios
we ride the GlamTram,
it conjures wonders for us;
icetunnels, flashfloods,
past the Orca, the WELCOME TO AMITY sign,

the giant shark attacks;
later I pose by his concrete carcase,
proud as Hemingway:
against a backdrop of the San Fernando Valley
brown in your white shorts
behind red-and-black umbrellas
you eat a frozen chocolate banana.

3

'*Entre Mobile
et Galveston.*' Between Santa Monica
and Venice Beach the musclemen
pump sunshine for you
in the iron heat. Palmtrees, breakdancers.
SEE CONAN THE DESTROYER written on the sky.
Today the airship saying FUJI FILM
that spied you there in your grey striped bikini
drifts aimlessly across the Mersey.

4

Guacamole. Ladies dressed like
embroidered postcards.
Mariachi bands, treelights.
Salsa Verde, Quesadas.
We celebrate your birthday with
Sangre de Toros.

5

At Disneyland
a huge blue bear waltzes you off
into Donald's Birthday Parade;

we are whirled in the dark
through artificial constellations;
on Tom Sawyer's raft
you perch on a keg of Dynamite
as the riverboat goes by.

6

Tears like New York summer rain
bleak lights beneath an awning
on Bleeker Street.

7

Graffiti city. Painted shadows
lurk round corners. Pakman, Gumby
haunt the walls. WORMS HAVE FIVE HEARTS
declares an East Village storefront.
Wanting to watch your name
on every train that goes by.

8

Harry the cat
stands on the back of the sofa
in the tiny room in Leroy Street,
scans us relentlessly.

9

In Washington Square
you stare entranced
at the squirrels.

Music in the darkened park:
tiny picnic-lights blossom,
effortless as skyscrapers.

11

In Bloomingdale's
you buy knickers with BLOOMIES on them;
JUNE IS LATEX LUST MONTH
says the sex-shop window on Times Square;
BLACK FLAG ROACH MOTEL
¡Las cucarachas entran
pero NO PUEDAN salir!
the subway-sign tells us;
The Caliente Cab Company
brings us frozen Margaritas;
Alexander Calder's
tiny metal circus-world
goes through its paces for you.

12

Last
late night drinks with Ed
goodbyes said
to Roscoe
in Kelly's, last place we go
on our way home
every night.

'I want to know what love is'
implores the muzak in the morning bank
'I want you to show me'

bright-eyed speedwell in a Cheshire field
forget-you-not

'Cryin Mr. Mailman
any mail for me today' Chicago blues
in windy city Liverpool

primrose and grey
walls of a Normandy bedroom
cliffs of Le Pollet, rockpools of Pourville

remember

The leaking tap in the bathroom
wheezes away to itself
like an old man dying.
Your white toothbrush still on the shelf,
Its white travelling-case no longer travelling,
spreads slowly like a dying sunflower
from a summer of neglect.

Tears like neon city rain

Lost sunset heights
of summer.

The Birthday Party

for Willy Russell

Happy Birthday, Dennis. Forty years, eh?
Talkin'bout my generation. Here's a present.
The latest John Denver: hope you haven't got it
already. What's that? Someone sent you
a fake bus pass? Probably those kids again. Typical.
Jane was saying only the other day
how well you looked. Thought you were never going
to ask. Not *red*? Hear that, Jane? Big Bold Burgundy . . .
Black mark. Sainsbury's. Gewurztraminer.
Here's looking at you, kid. Many of 'em.

You didn't think I'd forget, did you, Frank?
Spanish red. The man in Quicksave said it was all right.
What do you mean, you've stopped counting? Go on,
open it. Cheers. What? Oh, that. Yes,
I've done it: Compare and Contrast Shaw's *Pygmalion*
with *Educating Rita*. What do you mean, I can't say
I preferred *My Fair Lady*? You know, from the side
you look a bit like Michael Caine, Frank. If only
you'd smarten yourself up. Life begins at forty. Cheers.
Happy Birthday. Anyway, what's wrong with *My Fair Lady*?

I don't know. Lend us your lippy. Do you like it streaked
like this? Some feller's birthday. Sharon Louise from the office
told me. A writer or something. Funny thing to be.
Wonder what he does for a living? Quite dishy, really. For a
    writer.
Proper clothes and that. Giz a drink. Me seams straight?
    Cheers.
Wonder what the talent's like? Someone's fortieth, they
    reckon.
Forty. Bloodyell. It's like being an O.A.P. Hey,
what if all the tarts are his age? Grab-a-granny time.
Like a night down the Sausage Factory. Lend us your comb.
I'll wipe it after. What's this? Don Cortez. Cheers.

What's that, Mrs. Johnstone? They would have been forty
today?
Mustn't dwell on the past. Have another Guinness. Cheers.
Cheer up, it's a party. I don't know. Some writer feller.
Plays, someone said. Nice woman at the next table. Really
brown.
Says she lives in Greece. Wonder who she's talking to?
State of that one there. Supposed to be a teacher. Asleep under
the table. Nice girl with him, too. Ssh. They're making an
announcement . . .
Here's a Valentine from Shirley, and one from Rita, too,
a kiss from the Daughters of Albion, and a Birthday poem
    for you.

Ophelia

'There's rosemary, that's for remembrance:
pray you, love, remember . . .'

It is the painting I will not now paint for you.
Lying back in the upstairs bathroom
warm pink in a haze of warm water,
green with the essence of horse-chestnuts,
like the leaves hanging over her river.
1851, and in a golden summer
a man paints blue-flags, dog-roses, a robin
perched on a twig. Nearby, his friend paints a cornfield
not yet occupied by lovers. A willow dreams
aslant a brook. Look deep into the green world
of pondweed. In winter he will paint her
dress enchanted with tiny ornaments in a bathtub
in London. In Liverpool you would have floated
breasts above the water, pubic hair tangled
like water-crowfoot. Later I would have painted you
a Devon riverbank alive with dragonflies, valerian.
Viridian depths. This is the painting I would have made for
    you
my dark-haired, full-bodied Ophelia. But you are gone
and the image floats away downstream as shadows gather
in the green-carpeted bathroom. The lily-pads
of the bathmat you gave me remember.

Stakeout on High Street
for Richard Widmark and Samuel Fuller

bright lights on the jukebox
strings swoon into my favourite teenage popsong

again, this couldn't happen again . . .

his hard, cruel lips meet her full red ones
the blond sneering hoodlum
the brunette in the lownecked dress

streetlamps over the railwaybridge
tasting her lipstick all the way home

this is that once in a lifetime,
this is the thrill divine . . .

he slaps her hard across the face
black eyes gleam in the darkness
kisses her viciously again
resistance softens into passion

in a shelterhouse on the promenade
inexplicable soft shapes under the sweater

we'll have this moment for ever . . .

up the gangplank to his boat-house hideout
raincoat belted defiantly to the final shoot-out
cold eyes shadowed by his fedora

but never, never again

home, followed by the smell of cheap perfume
and the final showdown with tomorrow's homework.

Morning, Sunset Heights

Dogs bark
down the canyon.
A crow croaks
its complimentary
wake-u-up
croak-o-gram;
a hummingbird sips
from the hibiscus.
Bougainvillea
glows. The sun
hides behind thin mist
'Have a nice day'
ready on his lips.

Hollywood, California.

Morning, Liverpool 8

In Blackburne Place and Canning Street
the terraces half-wake,
stretch their balconies;
cast-iron railings, Ionic columns
blink into daylight from
a nightmare of bulldozers,
dripping water, charred beams,
distant dreams of hopscotch,
hoofbeats on cobblestones. The mirror tells
of a bright new face, does not reflect
the past neglect. Hope Place
and Huskisson tell of the nightmare
almost gone.

Misty Morning, Derbyshire

Plant strategies:
in a bloodless coup
dense shrubs have taken over the rockery,
isolated pockets of crocuses
hold out against the mist,
snowdrops scream their tiny defiance.
Reliance on an early spring
has over-extended the supply-lines;
the trees caught, leafless,
lifeless arms held high.

The hills have effected a strategic withdrawal.

Caller

In the time between
they pick it up
and put it down
I do it.
Quick syllables
slither down the line
like a hand up a skirt
on an escalator.
Sometimes I can hear
a little gasp of puzzlement
or fear. That's the best time.
Easy to please, that's me.
All it takes to satisfy
is 10p.

Suburban Landscape with Figures

Dusk. A suburban street. The smell
of lilacs. A man is walking
a small black-and-white dog.
At the corner it pauses, lifts a leg
against a fence, turns and focuses
its one good eye on the beloved master.
He pats it, absentmindedly.

Forced to see his grandfather's flesh
startled alive to his touch,
keeping him there in your head for ever;
all the nice young men,
the powdered bodies
propped carefully in armchairs,
placed carefully beneath floorboards,
long conversations in front of the telly
that never need a reply.

'They are not dead
but only sleeping'

Dusk. a suburban street. The smell
of lilacs. A man is walking
a small black-and-white dog.
At the corner it pauses, lifts a leg
against a fence, turns and focuses
its one good eye on the beloved master.
He pats it, absentmindedly.
In the flat he has just left, a pan
simmers on the gas-stove. In it,
a young man's severed head,
eyes incurious, bobs and bubbles.

Outside, shadows gather in the lilacs,
the buddleias.

Wish You Were Here

1

The amplified muezzin
calls the faithful at dawn;
the drunken and unfaithful
stir uneasily, go to sleep again.
The Taurus Mountains
sniff the air, paw the plain.
Car-horns bite like mosquitoes,
traffic-noise hangs in the air
like a heat-haze.

Izmir

2

A herd of goats, bells clanking,
runs
across a petrol-station forecourt.
A herd of tourists, cameras clanking,
runs
to photograph them.

Cappadocia

3

Like we sang
'All Things Bright and Beautiful'
dutiful schoolchildren
sing your songs
in the schoolhouse next door,
Garcia Lorca.

Casa Lorca, Fuentevaqueros

4

A Scouser in Spain
for James Fenton

'Hey, lad,
is there a Heladeria
round here?'

Granada

5

As she steps
into the sea
the waves froth at the mouth
with anticipation.

Sitges

6

We climb the monument
to The Unknown Vertigo Sufferer;
stone melting like cheese
supported on palm-trees,
supported on tortoises;
rosaries and foetuses,
palmleaf and acanthus,
rear from dripping shark-jaws
behind the jacaranda tree.

Sagrada Familia, Barcelona

7

One of the two
postcards I always sent
was to you:
now there's only one
to do.

8

Sparrows skirmish in the trees
above Achilles,
toppled stones
drenched in bloodred poppies;
puppies sleep in the sun
above the topless towers
of Ilium.

Troy

Domestic Interior

In the kitchen
she makes me a tree.
It tries to become a star
but fails.
It looks like a tree
trying to become a star.
It is made of cheese.

I eat it,
absentmindedly.

Outside,
the stars are turning into trees,
the trees are turning into cheese.

Visiting Writer

Sunday, and seven weeks
without a drink. I think of you
in another town. Outside, the leaves
turn brown. I think of me
rolling about someone's garden
like a bumblebee drunk on pollen
or tumbled laughing down a cobbled
Spanish hill. Still the birthday bruises
on my knee. I see your little student room
almost identical to this one. Summer gone,
and not a hangover to show for it.
Across the campus poems fall in September sunlight
like sober bells.

Four Studies of Dieppe
For the painter Nicholas Horsfield

I

light arrives in the harbour
like a monarch at a painter's door
the brush poised to trap
like a lobsterpot.

2

apple-orchards moult pink into summer
an excitement of melon against green lawns
the haze of sardines grilling
hydrangeas pushing in at the night window.

3

paint glitters like mackerel spilt on the quayside
the breath of ferries and fishingboats
caught against an impasto of cliffs
framed in an oval sunset.

4

burnt sienna scumbled against zinc white
where only the green-capped stones, gaunt as Frankenstein,
remember the suck of boots,
the crunch of landingcraft.

Crossing

They say it was written on her heart.
Calais. The warm wind smells of urine.
The spire beyond the bay.
Queen over the water, you're in
another country, now only inches away.
Seagulls scream through the chalk face of the page,
into a foreign day.

The Bell

The bell
tolled all afternoon
we did not send to ask
for whom.
It told of flowers
heaped in a goalmouth,
red and blue scarves
heaped together at an altar;
it told of
eyes like T.V. screens
haunted by last night's images,
tears dried by the April wind.
As the flags at half-mast
stirred overhead
the deep bell
still tolled in our heads
long after the light had gone.

Shadowland

This is Shadowland,
a place where nothing is as it seems:
a place of voices, faces from your dreams.
Who casts this shadow? What's behind that door?
What does the Weather Forecast have in store?
What lurks behind the Banham locks?
Who's that sleeping in a cardboard box?
What can you see through the double glazing?
Who's that gazing vacantly at the sky?

Government restrictions, unfortunately,
don't allow us to ask how or why.

In the interests of balance, of course, we have to say
that everything on the economic front
is great. The indicators indicate
an upward trend. What? You lost it all?
Don't worry, friend. It's just a blip,
a few percentage points. Everything points
to an upsurge. The F.T. 100, The Dow Jones,
bring words of hope and joy
through cordless telephones.

So step into this twilight world,
knock on any door. We're sure
you'll find it interesting.
Don't worry if the one you've picked
seems to be derelict. Call it
'Ripe for Improvement'. The whole movement's
towards conservation. Generous grants available.
It's all saleable; a whole nation for sale
with only history to offer; it's all the rage:
just dress it up and call it
Heritage.

Welcome to Shadowland!

It's the
GRAND BARGAIN
NEVER-TO-BE-REPEATED
DEEP-CUT ROCK-BOTTOM
SUPERSALE OF THE CENTURY!
Television, Radio,
everything must go!
Hospitals and science-labs,
everything's up for grabs,
even the water that you drink:
in fact, anything you can think of.
We're getting stronger: fresh air?
You won't get that for free much longer.
Don't worry if you find the payments hard.
No problem. Just use
your credit card.

*Voices. Voices from a dream. Voices that seem
as real as the person next to you on the bus.
Who's speaking? Them? You? Us?*

They lived next door for thirty years. *Years.*
By the time we heard the ambulance it was
too late. *Too late.* Anyway you don't like
to be nosy. *Nosy.* Not like some. *Some.*
Hanging over the gate to see. *See.* Catch me.
Catch me. Of course, we've always said 'Hello'.
'Hello'. A card through the letterbox at Christmas.
Christmas. How were we to know . . .

Waiting for Peter in Leicester Square. Why
isn't he there? Will Tinkerbell magic us away?
Will Mr. and Mrs. Darling say
'Come in lads, make yourselves at home'?
Home. A magic place as distant as
the Empire State. It's getting late.
The neon signs blink on in Never-Never Land.

Fed and changed like a babby.
Look at me. Neither use nor ornament.
Like a broken vase pushed to the back
of a shelf. An embarassment to them,
and myself. They'll be better off when I go.
Go where? The minutes, the seconds start.
So slow . . .

No marks out of ten, again.
The black marks pile up like shadows
on a winter afternoon. Soon they'll be back
asking questions I don't know how
to answer. Questions pile up
like fallen leaves. *You could be out there now,*
kicking through them under the streetlights.
Shadows lengthen like question-marks
in the empty classroom.

'Rockabye baby on the tenth floor
Mummy will hold you nice and secure
When Mummy breaks the cradle will fall
Down will come baby, Mummy and all'

Voices. Voices from a dream . . .

She stands, proud as Brittania,
rules the way we judge, and are judged.
She weighs us in her cold scales;
her ways mysterious, we do not see
what she weighs against us.
They say she's blind; I'm sure that's true;
be thankful: one of these days
she might turn her stony gaze
on you.

This is Shadowland. Is it just a nightmare?
Is it real? What are we supposed to feel?

And what are we supposed to do?
A twilight place where your worst dreams come true.
Frightened? Desperate? Confused?
Don't worry: it couldn't happen
to you.

For Joyce

'I don't want
to be any trouble' you'd say,
every day. 'Don't want
to be any trouble'. If you don't want
to be any trouble,
why do you walk into my dreams
every night?